I0516984

God
Whispers

Kevin B. Graham

TEL Publishing

God Whispers

For more information, please contact Kevin B. Graham

kevingraham711@gmail.com

Copyright © 2023 by Kevin B. Graham

Cover Design: Stephen Lursen, stephenlursen@gmail.com

Publisher: TEL Publishing

Publisher Contact: terrylursen@gmail.com

Starry Sky photo by Ivana Cajina Asuyh

Mountain Photo by Mads Schmidt Rasmussen

ISBN: 978-1-970094-07-7

All rights reserved. No part of this publication may be reproduced, or transmitted in any form, or by any means, electronic, mechanical, photocopying, recording, or otherwise without the prior written permission of the copyright owner.

Scripture taken from the King James Version of the Holy Bible unless noted otherwise.

Scripture taken from the NEW AMERICAN STANDARD BIBLE, © 1960, 1962, 1963, 1968, 1971, 1973, 1975, 1977, by the Lockman Foundation. Used by permission.

Scripture taken from the Berean Standard Bible, The Holy Bible, Berean Standard Bible, BSB Copyright ©2016, 2020 by Bible Hub. Used by Permission. All Rights Reserved Worldwide.

Library of Congress Cataloging-in-Publication Data

Graham, Kevin B., 1971-

God Whispers

Library of Congress Control Number: 2022923443

I dedicate this book to my loving wife, Monica, whose unwavering prayer and support for me has transformed and impacted me beyond words.

I love you Honey

With Special Thanks

To TEL Publishing, for premier excellence and unwavering accountability to authentic, heartfelt writing. Sir, I appreciate and honor the unspoken conviction of what it means to be a standard bearer.

To Jessica, and my grandchildren, your gentle hearts and caring spirits encourage me to believe you all still have that awesome imagination. Thank you Jessica, for Makeda and Noreace, I love you.

To Joshua, it is with great honor to be called your father, I love you with all my heart. You are a mighty and beautiful man that has changed my life forever. You are loyal, you are trustworthy, you have the heart of gold. Generations will be impacted by the very sound of your voice. You are chosen and marked for greatness. I love you son.

To Kirby, from the moment you were conceived, it was the conformation that heaven does hear our cry. You are destined to transform lives through sharing that joy everywhere you go. I love you.

Introduction

While writing this journal, and praying as I went along, oftentimes, it seemed as though I wanted a loud answer to my prayers, yet, God, in His own loving way and infinite wisdom would always whisper.

A whisper…a whisper is just that, it is to speak softly, using one's breath without one's vocal cords, especially for the sake of privacy.

So, I find it appropriate to this name writing, "God Whispers".

These writings have come out of a series of challenging private life events. There have been questions that I have longed for understanding, however, even when I didn't understand and while I couldn't share most of these things with other human beings, I begin to write my deepest heart's cry on paper, not realizing that my daily crisis led me to daily seeking God for answers.

It reminds me of when Elijah was in the cave dealing with multiple matters and the way he thought God would come, God didn't come. Instead, He came in a still small voice.

Many may find themselves in the loudness, or the busyness of their lives, however, in this journal we trust that you will find hope and strength and develop a hearing ear, not for the sonic boom, but for the still, small whisper of God. Let us take a journey in the questions, the promises, and the answers. Always pray. Always be praying as you read along…before, during, and after. It is my earnest desire that you will experience strength, hope, and comfort as you pursue deeper intimacy with God. May you hear His whisper.

Always pray,

Before, during, and after these daily readings.

"If my people, which are called by my name, shall humble themselves, and pray, and seek my face, and turn from their wicked ways; then will I hear from heaven, and will forgive their sin, and will heal their land." (2 Chronicles 7:14)

There is a Divine response that our God gives when He has received true worship. It's not forced, or manufactured. It is offered with a broken and contrite heart, a heart focused on the Father's love. God, who was with fire, responded to Solomon and then, after the fire of His presence, there was a reestablishment of the covenant with God and his chosen people Israel. This covenantal relationship had a divine and human responsibility.

God is waiting and desiring true intimacy with us. In this generation, will we respond with a heart of contrition in surrender, releasing sincere adoration to a loving God who is so deserving?

God wants His people who will willingly adhere to His requirement of true worship, not out of fear or a religious guilt, but out of a willingness of heart...in Spirit and in Truth.

If 'my' is a conditional word, how do you respond to the 'if' of God?

Have you been presented with an 'if' and how have you responded to the invitation to follow the instructions of God? Is this at your own convenience, or is it with a reckless abandon, forsaking your agenda for His desire?

God's word to you today…

"To my chosen one, I'm responding to your heart sacrifice and your reverence unto Me.

Let's continue in this divine romance, for I long to see my people respond to my directives for their own sake. It is My desire for My people to walk in harmony with Me for the purpose of revealing to the world that you are My people that are called by My name.

I have sought you and found you to reveal my splendor and Glory to a people that do not know My name. Will My people turn from the ways that hinder true kingdom advancement?

Turn to Me, My true worshipper. Allow Me to capture your heart this day, for you are the temple that I want to dwell in and the living sacrifice that I gladly receive."

Genesis 1:1, "And the earth was without form and void, and darkness was upon the face of the deep and the Spirit of God moved upon the face of the waters."

The Holy Spirit can make a glorious creation out of the most desolate place.

Our lives can parallel the creation story. The book of Genesis is the seedbed of all kingdom reality. We can take the principles from Genesis and build our lives on a solid foundation

"And the earth was without form…" The Hebrew word for form is "tohu" - meaning formlessness, confusion, unreality, and emptiness.

And I will walk with God…He understands the need for continual development to partake of His divine nature, but we must realize that the process of sanctification is ongoing.

God looked upon the earth and observed its chaos, however He was in the process of providing a solution.

Our Father knows the formless void…the chaotic dark areas of our lives, but the great news with a loving Father knowing all about you is that He has provided the Holy Spirit that comforts, and corrects; that purges, and heals and cleanses.

The Holy Spirit carried out God, the Father's, heart to bring order in the midst of formlessness.

What areas in your life need to be formed by the Holy Spirit?

He is our helper. He will comfort and complete us.

Present yourself before the Father; give Him your life and allow the Holy Spirit to breathe order, structure, strength, and light to every area that's needed.

"My child, I know the great things that I have in store for you. I see and understand the dark place that seems not to bear fruit, but fret not, for I did not make a mistake when I created you. I'm intimately involved in your formation. I'm holding you, molding you, and constructing you into the glorious image of my Son. You are not a mistake. For I will cause my Spirit to breathe upon you; to fill every void, to bring clarity where there's confusion and to bring light into the darkness. Stay pliable to my formation for I allow circumstances to form you. Although it's dark, I have the blueprint call on me and I will answer and I will show you great and mighty things that you do not know. I am birthing out of you My purpose, My plan, and My passion.

For though it's dark and formless, My Spirit is moving on your behalf. I know the plans that I have for you they are good and not of evil. I have the blueprint. Allow Me to build you according to My pattern."

Matthew 11:15, "He who has ears, let him hear."

Will you lend me your ear? "For my ways are not your ways, neither of my thoughts your thoughts…" Come away from the noise. Turn your attention to Me; for many have turned aside having itching ears, but I have clear instructions as you settle into my Presence.

For my people know my voice…the solution you prayed for is knocking at the door.

Are you attentive?

Remember, my way is peace, not confusion.

Peace, I give unto you.

Release the fear and lend me your ear.

Psalm 40:1, "I waited patiently for the Lord; and He inclined to me and heard my cry."

In this time of technology, the information age has created an environment of "right now!" However, a relationship with God has a different protocol. In the life of David, we are privileged to hear the heart of God's servant while he waits on the Lord.

Waiting in God's presence is a practice burst out of a period of time for God's personhood, not his performance. We desire Him for who He is, not what He can do for us. God desires true worship from your hearts.

God is not deaf, nor is he slow in his response. Every delay is not a sign of his displeasure.

My restless servant, have I not answered your prayer before…I'll never leave you, nor forsake you. What makes "now" any different?

Though it seems that there is a time of silence, I know all things and I'm inclined to hear your hearts cry. I'm with you; will you remain in a posture of thanksgiving…of gratefulness? Be of good cheer, for you are my child and I am your father.

Judges 2:1-5, "Now the angel of the LORD went up from Gilgal to Bochim and said, "I brought you up out of Egypt and led you into the land that I had promised to your fathers, and I said, 'I will never break My covenant with you, and you are not to make a covenant with the people of this land, but you shall tear down their altars.' Yet you have not obeyed My voice. What is this you have done? So now I tell you that I will not drive out these people before you; they will be thorns in your sides, and their gods will be a snare to you." When the angel of the LORD had spoken these words to all the Israelites, the people lifted up their voices and wept. So, they called that place Bochimb and offered sacrifices there to the LORD."

We live in a time now, I'll call it, the season of 10. God is always speaking. The number 10, in the Hebrew, means the hand of God. The Hebrew pictures God's hand, or God's fist.

God explains human responsibility during this time. God has a prescribed way for humanity. Humanity is responsible for carrying out God's rule for his purposes in the earth.

10 is a time of probation. 10 is a tithe; the human responsibility.

When Moses was giving the Ten Commandments, God was establishing a culture, a royal nation of holy people that would transform the world as we knew it. However, God's plan for me is what is consistently hindered due to human disobedience.

The cycle in the book of Judges is this: God will give a command. Man will not walk in it. Man will worship idols. God will send an enemy. God's people will cry out to Him. Then, God will send a prophet, a leader, a judge, and a remnant of the people will return to Him in obedience and God will deliver them.

This was a constant cycle in Old Testament reality. This cycle parallels society. We are at a place where there needs to be a cry unto God and a response from God's prophetic people to carry the heart and mind of God to a lost and dying people.

In this time, this is a clarion cry from God's heart for God's people to follow Christ in uncertain territories.

Are you willing to forsake house, man, career, wealth, riches?

This is ministry for the Life of Christ. God is reestablishing His first priority in the life of those that will realign themselves for His original purpose for humanity.

Isaiah 43:19, "Behold, I am about to do something new. Even now it is coming. Do you not see it?"

To my transitioning children I know the way that you should go for I have prepared a way that you should dwell.

I'm not lost, neither are you. For I shall give you strength in the desert and clarity in your foggy day. Allow me to bring you into a place of peace and comfort.

For I will sustain each step that you take as a loving father comforts a child who's learning how to walk.

I will hold you and make sure that your steps will land on solid ground.

My word is a lamp to your feet and a light to your path.

You grope for the night place…I am the light…walk in this light and be comforted. Although it is new to you, it's normal for me.

I am the first and the last, the beginning and the end.

Abide in my promise, for I am now bringing you into a place not common to your experience.

Mark 4:35, "On the same day, when evening had come, He said to them, "Let us cross over to the other side.'"

Have you ever received a call that was unexpected in the evening time? Well, I have, and sometimes my heart stops with anticipation of what may happen on the other end of that call. Questions arise, "Is it good news, bad news, is everything okay?" I'm not sure, so with great apprehension I respond and answer the call.

At the time of this new discipling process with Christ and his followers, He had just taught on the parables of the kingdom of God. Just when the crowd was around and there was a great response, Christ gave a command to tell his disciples, "Let's cross over to the other side."

Christ has such a way to keep us in pursuit of Him so that we may not rest on past events, pressing the kingdom of God forward.

It was imperative that our Lord transition His students to the other side.

I'm calling you to the other side, to walk in the journey with your eyes on me. Understand that I know the end from the beginning. Allow me to be revealed in you for the purpose of manifesting my teaching in you. As you move from the familiar into the unknown, understand that I am your Good Shepherd. I will lead and guide you to a destination that's for good and not for evil. Rely on me through my word as I get you to the water of life. I've never lost a passenger and I won't start with you, for you are mine and I will see you through.

Learn to trust my nature, whether you see a sign, or not. For in my still, small voice, you will be strengthened and comforted. Focus not on the storms, nor the winds, or the waves. Continue in true worship. I make all things work together for your good.

Matthew 14:22, "And straightway Jesus constrained his disciples to get into a ship, and to go before him unto the other side, while he sent the multitudes away."

When following Jesus, there will be instructions given that you may not understand right away.

After witnessing the miracle of provision, Jesus instructed the disciples to embark on a new journey, which required a change of location with a different mode of transportation

Embark means to get aboard a ship and begin a course of action.

Come with me, my excited disciple. Although you have seen many great wonders and the demonstration of my provision, I have more for you. Come with me to the other side of my redemptive plan, for I am now taking you into territory that is unfamiliar to the status quo.

Commit to hearing and obeying my voice, for this journey will impact a people for a particular purpose.

Galatians 6:9, "And let us not be weary in well doing: for in due season we shall reap, if we faint not."

There are times in life when I question my purpose, calling, and reason for living. In my finite mind, I'm fighting to grasp the understanding of it all. Oftentimes, I outwardly showing pseudo strength, all the while crumbling under the pressure of performance.

Oh, I am absolutely exhausted and frustrated, sometimes to the point of throwing in the towel. Have you ever been in this place? Well, you're not alone in this journey that we call life. We will experience highs and lows, barriers and bondage, along with the wheat and tares, and the toils and snares.

We build our lives according to our passions. In pursuit of our purpose, we will experience certain levels of fatigue - mentally, spiritually, and physically.

If we are born anew into Him, God has promised to be with us no matter how we feel. I'm convinced that He's really waiting for you to acknowledge Him. While you're tired, His promise for us is that He'll never leave us nor forsake us.

What is your focus in the time of weariness? Is it centered on self or centered in God?

Dear weary worshiper, I know that you're weary, but be of good cheer, I will strengthen you in grace. You to finish the course!

Don't look to the left nor to the right. Look unto me, the author and the finisher of your faith. I shall comfort you in this time of weariness, for my strength is made perfect in times like these.

I give words of instructions to you that will uphold you and bring you a place of tranquility.

Maintain your godly character and I will reward you in the midst of it all.

Remember my child, the words that I whisper in your heart, come unto me all ye that are heavy laden and I will give you rest.

Rest in me. Take all the toil and roll your cares on me. These matters are too big for you, so give them to me and I will care for you and comfort you; for you are my child and I will see you through.

Job 10:1-4, "I loathe my very life; therefore I will give free reign to my complaint and speak out in the bitterness of my soul. I say to God: Do not declare me guilty, but tell me what charges you have against me. Does it please you to oppress me, to spurn the work of your hands, while you smile on the plans of the wicked"

Things happen that challenge our faith. Questions arise and cause us to wrestle with what we believe. Wrestling with your faith isn't a sign of weakness, but evidence of your humanity. The men and women in the Bible reveal this to us.

Don't be surprised when your faith is challenged to a wrestling match. The Bible tells us to fight the good fight of faith. Winning a good faith wrestling match can make you stronger.

Dear frustrated warrior, I have not forgotten your labor of love.

I've seen your tears and heard your frustrated heart.

Focus on me, for I am your guide, comfort, and your source of wealth.

Do not forget whose you are in the assignment I have commissioned for you. Arise from your cave and go into the attitude of thanksgiving for my thoughts for you are good and not evil. Remember the day I called you. I have never left you nor have I forsaken you; so, be of good courage. Receive my comfort and recover all for I am not through with you; we have only just begun.

People, my measurement of your success has nothing to do with the philosophies of man, but in the place of obedience.

Turn your heart to me and I shall fill you with the grace and truth and understanding needed to complete the task. Peter, John, and Elijah are a few who became frustrated in the times of fulfilling their purpose. I did not let them down, neither shall I let you down.

Psalm 138:8, "The LORD will fulfill His purpose for me. O LORD, Your loving devotion endures forever—do not abandon the works of Your hands." (BSB)

Verse Concepts:

1) The Lord will accomplish what concerns me;
2) Your lovingkindness, O Lord, is everlasting;
3) Do not forsake the works of Your hands.

This is the decade of the hand of God

Oh, LORD, do not forsake us!

He Is…Accomplishing careers

He Is…Guidance

He Is…His Promises

Destiny Schedules Man, this is the Creation of Goals.

My beloved son and daughter, whom I've created by my own hand, I found you intentionally to commune uninterrupted with me. Did I not promise that I will never leave you nor forsake you? Because we are one, I am your loving father and I change it not. I have known you from your beginning and though you're in a tough time, my presence is with you and has gone before you. Remember that I have begun a great work in you and I shall complete it!

You are not alone for I am forever with you. I will uphold you; I will sustain you. Call on me and I will show you great and mighty things. For you are my choice, designed by my hand. No situation or circumstance can pull you out of my hand.

As I revealed my Glory to Moses through my commandments, I was showing divine revelation for my people to have human responsibility. I release my grace unto a people to respond to my leading and although I have gone before you, there are still responsibilities and corresponding action to my directions for your life.

Isaiah 4:10, "Fear not for I am with thee, be not dismayed. for I am thy God. I will strengthen thee, yes, I will help thee. I will uphold you with the right hand of my righteousness."

In times of transition, you will experience fears. As we enter the new seasons of our lives, there will be uncertainties that have the possibility to create anxiety.

However, there is comfort in the words of God to you in the time of transition of moving from one place to the next. We sometimes have questions like why, what, when, or where. If you've ever asked these questions, welcome to the time of transition. Don't panic, don't lash out. Get into a place of solitude and posture your heart to hear these words.

Fear not. Imagine a father at the swimming pool with his children encouraging them to enter the water, but the children have apprehension. Although they want to experience the joy of being in the water, they must be encouraged not to fear the very thing they desire to enter.

The father has made a way for his children to experience the swimming pool, however the child must hear the father's comforting voice saying, "Don't fear, I'm right here with you."

Where you have fears, the Father is saying, "Fear not, you're not alone, you're not abandoned. You are protected, covered, and supported by my hand. I shall release peace that will guard your heart and mind for you are my children and I will release love that's perfect and my perfect love will cast out all fear. So, lean not to your own understanding. Trust me, that I'm able to catch you before you fall. I have postured you to experience my abundant Joy. You will not falter, for I am with you."

What are some areas of your life where fear has kept you from entering what the Father has prepared for you?

As a father of three, I've experienced the interaction a father and his children. There were times when my son wanted to go to the water park and his greatest desire was to slide down the water slide into the pool. Yet, as he ascended to the top of the water slide, I'd notice that he kept looking back at his father step by step. We made eye contact and with a gentle move of my hand, I encouraged him to continue to go onward after reaching the top of the slide. He began his descent into the water with great speed and he entered the pool of water at the bottom landing on his back and what was supposed to be joy, turned into sheer panic!

My son began to cry, "Help, help! I'm drowning, I am drowning!" I saw him lying on his back in the water and my reply to my son was, "Stand up son, you're not drowning. You're taller than the water that you're swimming in! Stand up, and you will be above the water."

The pool of water he had landed in was only two feet deep, but it was his perspective that allowed fear to grip his heart. Out of this lesson, I want to encourage you.

You are not drowning, you will not die, nor shall you perish. Stand up because you are bigger than what you're facing. Change your position. Take a chance for your heavenly Father is right here with you to remind you that you are greater than what you're swimming in. Rise up, be of good courage, because your heavenly Father is backing you.

Jeremiah 33:3, "Call on me and I will answer and show you great minded things that you know not of."

When will we tire of self-willed self-sufficient egomania? God wants a relationship with us.

Oftentimes, we wait on others to reach out to us to prove their loyalty and care in the relationship. However, we must become honest, open, and willing to become vulnerable enough in the relationship to call upon that reliable source. Will you move beyond your own self-centeredness and call on God today?

I'm so glad that you chose to call me. I have longed for you to turn your heart totally over to me that I may respond in a manner that's conducive to your total transformation.

Now that your posture is that of a student waiting for the teacher to teach, I now show you clarity. I silence the internal argument that opposes my original intention for you. My creation is good and I make no mistakes about what I created. You are my masterpiece. I give you the gift of hearing my voice that produces My peace that surpass all man's understanding. Welcome to My Kingdom.

1 Peter 5:7, "Casting all your care upon him; for he cares for you."

I can imagine Peter walking with Christ in the beginning, trusting in his talent, ability, and experience as a fisherman. Christ, being the skillful teacher that he is, had to cause learning by relating to his students' field of knowledge in fishing.

Jesus explained the kingdom by way of parable and demonstration. The measurement of this teaching would show up later after the death of Christ in Peter's writing. He used a fishing analogy in his message to the early believers teaching them how to cast their cares. Peter knew how to cast nets. This term means 'to throw upon swiftly'. Peter exhorts the believer to swiftly throw their cares upon a trustworthy Christ who can bear all things.

Cast all your cares upon me, for caring not transferred becomes bondage. Throw all fears, doubts, and personal matters on me, for my yoke is easy and my burden is light. These cares distract you from living, moving, and having your constant fellowship with me.

Casting is the way prescribed for maintaining the peace of mind and stability of heart that you seek.

Don't be held captive to the thoughts that take you away from my presence, but take action. Release all of your thoughts to me as they come. I am your peace. Your burden will become my burden as you cast it on to me.

Genesis 28:13, "Look, I am with you, and I will watch over you wherever you go, and I will bring you back to this land. For I will not leave you until I have done what I have promised you." (BSB)

You may not be able to see it and other people may not be able to acknowledge it, but God is up to something great in your life today. While you're driving to work, or while you're sitting at your desk at the computer, you could be trying to figure out the wisdom of God. Will you find it in the world? The wisdom of God means applied knowledge. The Divine wisdom of God will give you the Divine instruction that you need.

Know that I've cried out to you…why are you losing sleep, why are you fighting this? If I brought you through one thing, I will bring you through another. I am a God that cannot lie. I have spoken a word of strength over you, I have spoken a word of healing over you; I have spoken it.

Our God is the god of the 12th hour, though it seems like you had a Lazarus situation here to tell you your situation may look dead, but God is seated from another perspective. The instance when Jesus came on the scene and His very mother was concerned, you have to take an approach like her, "I'm going to take God at His word."

Do you know that God is not moved because of the coronavirus? God is moved by faith. God is not moved by the presidential election. God has not been moved by different affections; God is moved when he hears a praise on your lips. How many people can thank God midst of the praise? God is in the midst of the test. Thank God though you're getting worried, He will bring you strength and a new season is coming for you right now. There's a new strength coming for you right now. I know that, by the power of the Holy Spirit, God is reaching out to you. He is reaching out to you, child. Trust in God. Give God one more time of praise. I dare you to bless God right now where you are. I dare you to bless Him with all that is within you… bless His Holy Name!

Pruning season

John 15:1-2 says, "I am the true vine, and my father is the gardener. Every branch in me that that does not bear fruit he takes away, and every branch that does bear fruit he prunes, that it may bear more fruit."

There are times when things are going well; there is peace and harmony, there is abundance and there is stability in your relationship with God, self, and others. Then, out of nowhere, it seems like a time of loss, subtraction, frustration, and friction.

Our minds begin to question, "Why is this happening? Did I do something wrong? Am I being punished?"

In times like these, we must not lean to our own understanding, but seek God's word for comfort, wisdom, and understanding.

The scriptures teach us about pruning. When we get the mindset of Christ being a true vine and the Father being the gardener, it gives us vivid imagery of our lives abiding in the Life of Christ.

In gardening, there is a process called pruning, whereby the good parts of a plant are periodically cut back to ensure structural integrity and healthy growth in the life of the plant.

Can you see how God loves us so much that He will cut back seemingly great things, not because of anger, but for the development of Christ's nature in you to ensure the structural integrity of your heart. The plant never argues with how it is being shaped, or groomed. Its responsibility is to abide.

At this time of cutting away in your life, abide in the truth of God's word and His ability to care for everything that concerns you.

To my beloved child, count it not strange when experiencing loss, set back, or suffering, for I am the gardener who's cutting the disease, the ill-formed and the dysfunctional areas of your life that hinders fruitfulness.

I've allowed reduction to maintain form and structural integrity in all things being done in my name.

This is not punishment, for I love you enough to make sure that your growth is healthy and consistent. This cutting back is a redirection and protection to ensure a great harvest that shall come forth.

Luke 4:18, "The Spirit of the Lord is upon me, because he hath anointed me to preach the gospel to the poor; he hath sent me to heal the brokenhearted, to preach deliverance to the captives, and recovering of sight to the blind, to set at liberty them that are bruised."

The ministry of Christ on the earth was a pattern for future ministers of Christ to follow. Christ, which means the anointed one, and His anointing reveals to us the need for the Holy Spirit's empowerment to fulfill God's mandate to broken humanity.

Jesus, after being tested and tried in the wilderness, made a bold proclamation concerning why the Spirit of God was upon him. The Holy Spirit is our helper to enforce what Christ came to fulfill.

The Holy Spirit empowered Jesus to carry out the mission of proclaiming the good news with demonstration of power.

I remember my first stages of ministry, I would encounter the Holy Spirit in ways that the scriptures talk about, yet I did not know that this was the beginning of a partnership with Holy Spirit.

Why is it important to be anointed for ministry? The person of the Holy Spirit confirms the words of Christ.

Christ's earthly ministry was full of the demonstration of grace. This grace means divine, enabling power to accomplish His mission.

Are you in dwelling in the power of the Holy Spirit? We must seek God for the empowerment of the Holy Spirit in our everyday life, as well as carrying out the commission of Jesus Christ.

May you find the power source for the fulfillment of Christ's mission on the earth.

To my chosen ones, I shall pour out my Spirit upon all, for I have need of you to proclaim my good news; to teach my word, and to carry out my commission with the power needed to establish my kingdom. I know you this day to accomplish all that I've put your hands to, for is not by power, nor by might, but it's by my Spirit. Walk in my Spirit so that you may not fulfill the lust of the flesh. I'm pouring out upon you this day a new anointing that will bring you into alignment with my purpose.

Isaiah 61:4, "They will rebuild the ancient ruins; they will restore the places long devastated; they will renew the ruined cities, the desolations of many generations." (BSB)

Isaiah, through the inspiration of the Holy Spirit, begin to declare the future freedom of God's chosen people while they were still in their present bondage. Life has a way of showing you one thing when God's purposes are totally above that. Isaiah's purpose was to paint a future hope of God's chosen people in the midst of ruins, dilapidation, and demise. God had forgiven His people's rebellion, but there were consequences to this rebellion.

Later, when the children of Israel returned home from captivity, they found a new normal: death, destruction, and the decay of Jerusalem. It seems that when God graces us to repent, we must go to the process of recovery. This is not a one-stop miracle. This process is a life-long process of building, raising, and repairing that which was lost while being in captivity. We now see in Isaiah the solution in the nature of restoration that comes through Christ, the anointed one.

God's method was to send His Son to redeem His people and commission His people to build to raise and repair the ruined cities, symbolic of people, places, and things.

I am one who has received the chastening of God, the mercy of God, and the restoration of God. I now have been commissioned to be an extension of Christ's life that brings restoration throughout humanity.

For this is the time that I am calling you into action, for I have brought you out of captivity to release you back to your promise place.

Though the task seems great, I am with you, for you will build according to my pattern. How long should you build outside of me? I am the one with the blueprint. Build according to my plan and my purpose for your life.

I am increasing the level of your strength and position and bringing addition to your life for my purpose and my glory to be revealed. I now summon you into action. I have used you in times before to create a disturbance for the disruption of captivity. My grace is now extended to your life for putting back together the broken things. I'm replacing the old way of doing it and putting together what has been torn and broken. As I have forgiven, strengthened, and made amends with you, sit up straight and right the relationships that I have blessed you with. For I am now ready for you to be the instrument that will build, raise, and repair the ruined places.

Man's Limitations Meets God's Ability

Ephesians 3:20, "Now unto him that is able to do exceedingly, abundantly above all that we ask or think, according to the power that worketh in us."

God's ability far exceeds man's ability, however, God's ability in man is only released by man surrendering his will to God.

Grace is God's ability working in and through us.

I've come to understand that surrender to God means dropping all excuses and self-defense mechanisms that keep us dependent upon our own intellect, talents. and abilities. All of these things have their limits. When life's challenges meet man's limitations, men and women must realize that someone far greater than themselves is in control of their circumstances.

Human need is God's opportunity to show Himself Mighty.

There was a time in my life when I depended on my own self will, yet I became a prisoner to the thoughts and fears of other people, places, and things. I found myself caught in a vicious cycle of fear, dishonesty, guilt, and shame due to trusting the ego's limited faculties. This cycle could not break until I became honest with myself, with God, and with others.

I had to acknowledge my human frailty when it came to coping with life's ever-changing situations and circumstances. Feeling broken inside, I turned my will over to God, and to my surprise, I experienced a strength, peace, and comfort that I never knew existed. Now I get it! It was a grace encounter, after humbling myself to God's ability to do for me what I could not do for myself.

Grace be unto my servant who has found rest me. For I have longed for this time of rest for you, however, self-will, ego and self-protection has kept my servant in a constant cycle of deceit, frustration, and discouragement.

I have seen your toil. I have heard your cry. I extend to you this day peace, and safety for you have now surrendered your will for my purposes.

Although your ability is limited, you will come to know that my ability far exceeds any human efforts; for I am your God, your strength, and my grace is available to the humble.

Psalm 126:1-6, A song of ascents, "When the LORD brought back the captives to Zion, we were like men who dreamed. Our mouths were filled with laughter, our tongues with songs of joy. Then it was said among the nations, "The LORD has done great things for them." The LORD has done great things for us, and we are filled with joy. Restore our fortunes, O LORD, like streams in the Negev. Those who sow in tears will reap with songs of joy. He who goes out weeping, carrying seed to sow, will return with songs of joy, carrying sheaves with him.

There's nothing like being released from the things that have held you captive. A captive is one being held like a prisoner, or, in confinement like an animal.

In this writing, we experience the gratitude to God for past and future redemption. Israel had become captive to the Babylonians due to their self-will and rebellion against God.

I have learned in my life and walk with God that when I resist God's authority, I find myself forced to submit to unrighteous authority, thus, having to deal with people, places, and things that are not God's best for me. The fruit thereof is fear, unrest, and confusion. I believe that all fear is disloyalty to God. It is a denial of His care and protection.

God is a loving God. He has patience. However, there are consequences when God's chosen people refuse to follow his path and those consequences can lead to captivity, or sometimes, death.

Captivity changes your mindset, your appetite, and your productivity.

The children of Israel, God's chosen people, were forced to be subject to unjust, cruel behavior until they cried out to Him.

It's comforting to know that, although God corrects those that He loves, His ear is still open to the cry of a repentant heart. I have called out to the Lord in the times when our relationship was distant or strained due to my waywardness, and God heard the cry of my heart. He released me from the captivity of my oppressor and placed me in a place of grace.

My people, who are called by My name, I will set the captives free when repentance is found in their hearts. I shall restore your peace and restore your health when I have seen your tears. I have heard your cry, though you stayed in unfamiliar places. I will show you the way to the place of grace. Look up, for your redemption is here!

I have received the seed of your tears. You shall reap a strength that has come out of the process of correction. Know that I correct them that I love. I love you in spite of where you've been, and I love you too much to let you stay there. This day, I will put a song of liberation in your heart and you will declare to my people that I am the God who does great things for them.

Matthew 26:39, "And He went a little beyond them, and fell on His face and prayed, saying, "My Father, if it is possible, let this cup pass from Me; yet not as I will, but as You will."

God has a plan for our lives, we hear this often, but what is the cost behind the prayer, "Thy will be done"?

Oftentimes, I battle between my will and God's way and wisdom. By nature, human beings are self-willed.

I'm really beginning to see how much of my will overrides God's will. One day I surrender my will only to take my will back the next minute.

"Oh, God, help me to surrender, for I do not know how to fight between my ego and surrendered living."

Ego edging God out has been a constant battle in my life. I now accept that I'm not in control of other people, places, or things. I'm willing to allow God to take the driver seat. It's not my mind, but the mind of Christ; it's not my life, but Christ's life within me; it's not my will, but Thy will be done.

My child, let go of the attachments that weigh you down. Release them unto me. For my burden is easy and surrender sets you free. Although you grieve over the matter that's released, I'm still the God of all comfort and through me, I provide you peace.

Rely and trust in my perfect plan, for no one has ever been taken from my hand. Abide in me, and I will abide in you. Allow my divine plan to shine bright in and through you.

Isaiah 60:11, "Your gates shall be open continually; day and night they shall not be shut, that people may bring to you the wealth of the nations, with their kings led in procession." (ESV)

What an awesome passage of scripture. This promise of God is for the people of God. In this prophetic promise, we see the word "gate".

This promise was concerning a gate being open continually. If we read this casually, we will overlook this gate, but let's uncover the meaning of this promise.

A gate was very significant in Biblical times because it was most important to the territory where they lived. Throughout scripture we see where business took place; elders would sit at the gate to judge.

Many of the battles to be won must be won at the gate.

In Acts 12:10, it says, "When they had passed the first and second guard, they came to the iron gate that leads into the city which opened for them by itself and they went out and went along one street and, immediately the angel departed from them."

My children, I have opened gates unto you this day. Divine access has been given to long-standing obstacles and blockages. What was once considered closed is now open unto you. I've heard your prayers and supplications. Rejoice, for I am the God who has opened the gates and granted divine access.

Romans 8:19, "For the earnest expectation of the creature waits for the manifestation of the sons of God."

Sonship comes with inheritance in partaking of the divine nature of God through Christ Jesus.

> *"Joy to the world the Lord has come,*
>
> *let earth receive her King.*
>
> *Let heaven and nature sing; let heaven and nature sing."*

The verse in this song speaks to me even as a child singing this Christmas song. It moves me in a special way. I did not understand the significance of this verse until I entered a personal relationship with Christ and being adopted into the family of God through Jesus Christ. God has given His Son, Jesus, a name that is above all names. It is true that at that name, every knee shall bow, in heaven and in earth. The supremacy of Jesus is revealed in the heavens and in the earth, formed by Christ, was all things created and apart from Him nothing was created. (John 1).

The order of God is revealed in John 3:16, "For God so loved the world (the cosmos, the orderly arrangement of things), that he gave his only begotten son, that whosoever believes in Him shall not perish, but have everlasting life."

God loves the orderly arrangement of all things. We see this in the book of Genesis, or what we call the 'book of beginnings.' In seven days, God ordered how often nature should operate. In understanding the glory of the seasons, we know when the changes take place in the landscape. Flowers know when it's time to bloom and animals understand when it's time to migrate.

However, man was found out of alignment to God's orderly

arrangement due to the fall in the garden, releasing chaos in the earth. With this fall, God's prize possession, man, had to be released from his place of dominion and glory, to a place of toil. The earth responded to man's disobedience and to God by manifesting thorns as God commanded.

God is all-knowing and has predetermined a solution for fallen man through Christ, His Son, and our King. Through Christ we have now received the spirit of adoption whereby we cry, "Abba, Father." He Is Christ in us, the hope of glory, being revealed throughout the day.

Today, surrender in total obedience to Christ teachings. Let us rejoice for being made sons of God and in Him establishing Christ's reign and rule in the earth.

Oh, my beloved sons, in whom I am well pleased, walk in the liberty whereby My Son, Jesus, has made you free. Don't be entangled again with the yoke of bondage. I have brought you to the table to dine at my feast. You are my prized possession. Walk in your inheritance and occupy until I come.

Hebrews 3:15-19, "While it is said,

"TODAY IF YOU HEAR HIS VOICE, DO NOT HARD-EN YOUR HEARTS, AS WHEN THEY PROVOKED ME."

For who provoked Him when they had heard? Indeed, did not all those who came out of Egypt led by Moses? And with whom was He angry for forty years? Was it not with those who sinned, whose bodies fell in the wilderness? And to whom did He swear that they would not enter His rest, but to those who were disobedient? So, we see that they were not able to enter because of unbelief." (Berean Study Bible)

Will you pray this prayer of confession…

Dear God,

My heart is hardened to the trial and tribulations of life. My hope is gone and hearing your voice is a thing of the past. I'm walking in the wilderness of unanswered questions; drowning in my own self-centeredness.

I'm lost in the cloud of false hopes and dashed dreams that allow me to justify my disobedience. Anger towards You seems easier than accepting the truth about my own character flaws.

The stone of doubt, fear, anger, and unbelief has lodged in my heart during times of trauma.

I come to you broken, afraid, and tired. To You, oh, God, I turn my will and life over to Your care because You are able to remove these stones in my heart.

Holy Spirit, You are welcome into this trauma and dysfunction. Make the crooked places of my heart straight and this stony heart, a heart of flesh. Breathe Your life into me.

My child, surrender your stony heart unto Me, for I am able to give you a new heart and the right perspective. You're not abandoned, nor are you fatherless. I understand the pain and frustration expressed in this time of uncertainty. I am here. I was there and will always be present in your life. Take My hand of comfort, as I skillfully reconstruct your love, for this is the day of new beginnings.

Psalm 150:6, "Let everything that hath breath praise the Lord. Praise ye the Lord."

Pray this as a prayer and sing it as a praise…

"Oh Lord, I praise You. Be glorified in all that was, that is, and that is to come. You alone deserve all the glory, all of the Honor, and of the praise. May heaven and nature bow at Your majesty for great is our God and greatly to be praised. In distress, I've made Your name my hiding place for in Thee, my heart is established. There is no one like my King. Waters have to be parted in the seas of impossibility. Lions are calmed at the sound of worship released from the throne room. Oh, come, let us testify of your loving kindness and tender mercies. From age to age, the generations declare the goodness of our King Jesus. May the earth ring out with reverence unto the spotless, sinless Lamb of God. Praise Him all you people; praise heavenly host, praise Him all creation. Let everything that has breath, praise the Lord."

For I delight and dwell in the praises of my people. This praise is displayed from a sincere heart that drives Me into every situation and circumstance in the praise-filled life. For in praise, battles are won, the impossible becomes the possible and walls fall down before My power.

I have heard your praise and I respond with My favor and strength. Rejoice, for I am in the midst of those who praise from the place of Spirit and Truth.

John 14:6, "Jesus saith unto him, I am the way, the truth, and the life: no man cometh unto the Father, but by me."

Christ is the course we travel to God, the route taken to everlasting life. He said these things about Himself:

I am sent from God.

I am the street to walk on in the kingdom of heaven.

I am the only Way to the Heavenly Father.

I am the truth and the life. "No one comes to the Father except through Me." The "I am" here is the first of seven self-descriptions of Jesus introduced by "I am" and echoes Exodus 3:14, where God said, "I am who I am — tell them the 'I am' has sent me (Moses) to you."

Please read this account of Moses and the burning bush in Exodus, Chapter 3. We all need to realize and know that Jesus is not only the "Son of man" and the Son of God, He also is God Himself. The blessed Trinity, God the Father, God the Son, and God the Holy Spirit — the three in one. Jesus further said that He is the Way — this means He is the way to God.

way, manner, mode, form, style, modus

δρόμος

road, street, way, route, path, course

διαδρομή

route, way, course, journey, trip

I am the journey taken to get to the Father. I am the path of eternal life; the road of redemption by My ultimate sacrifice. Follow Me, I will make you fishers of men; placing souls on the street called Straight. I am, Christ within you, the hope of Glory...the course that men must take.

John 10:1-3, "Truly, truly, I tell you, whoever does not enter the sheepfold by the gate, but climbs in some other way, is a thief and a robber. But the one who enters by the gate is the shepherd of the sheep. The gatekeeper opens the gate for him, and the sheep listen for his voice. He calls his own sheep by name and leads them out." (Berean Study Bible)

GOD has given the "gates of the enemy" to us by a PROMISE!

What happens at the GATES?

Especially in ancient times, GATES were the MOST important part of CITY! Gates were the "traffic control" stations of those coming IN and OUT.

GATES were the gathering places of people.

Business was conducted at the gates (remember the story of Ruth). Important NEWS was proclaimed at the GATES.

Kings and elders sit at the GATES to pass judgement.

Judges 5:8, says, "When Israel chose new gods, war erupted at the city gates. Yet not a shield or spear could be seen among forty thousand warriors in Israel!"

We see that WHOEVER sits at the GATES, controls that territory!

Y'shua (Jesus) said He IS the ONLY GATE...salvation, deliverance, and healing are decided at the gates and only comes through Him.

Verily, verily, I say unto you, except a man be born again, he cannot see the kingdom of God.

Migratory Behavior - "And you came near and stood at the foot of the mountain, while the mountain burned with fire to the heart of heaven, wrapped in darkness, cloud, and gloom. Then the LORD spoke to you out of the midst of the fire. You heard the sound of words, but saw no form; there was only a voice. And he declared to you his covenant, which he commanded you to perform, that is, the Ten Commandments, and he wrote them on two tablets of stone. And the LORD commanded me at that time to teach you statutes and rules, that you might do them in the land that you are going over to possess." (Deuteronomy 4:11-14, ESV)

The phenomenon of migration has been in existence for centuries and is driven by aspects of economics, natural disasters, social-political factors, demographic increase and urbanization, wars and family reunification factors. Migration is also called a process of people adapting to a new environment which involves making decisions, preparations, going through the procedures, shifting physically to another geographical area, adjusting to the local cultural needs and becoming a part of the local system.

A mountain symbolizes constancy, permanence, motionlessness, and at its peak spiritually signifies the state of absolute consciousness.

The spiritual meaning of a mountain is often associated with consistency, inspiration, spiritual awakening and overcoming obstacles. Mountains symbolize progress and having the mental strength to overcome the challenges you're currently facing or have faced in the past.

What type of behavior is migration?

Migration is an innate behavior characterized as the long-range seasonal movement of animals; it is an evolved, adapted response to variation in resource availability.

Internal migration: moving within a state, country, or continent

External migration: moving to a different state, country, or continent

Emigration: leaving one country to move to another

Immigration: moving into a new country

Return migration: moving back to where you came from

Seasonal migration: moving with each season or in response to labor or climate conditions

What are three reasons that humans migrated?

People migrate for many reasons, ranging from security, demography, and human rights to poverty and climate change. A significant number of immigrants have had previous, recent, and/or ongoing experiences with trauma. Traumatic experiences place immigrants at risk for mental health problems, including depression and anxiety disorders, and particularly post traumatic stress disorder.

What are the five stages of migration? There are five common migration approaches: Retire, Replace, Rehost, Rearchitect, and Retain.

You've been at this mountain long enough!

Deuteronomy 8:2, "You shall remember all the way which the Lord your God has led you in the wilderness these forty years, that He might humble you, testing you, to know what was in your heart, whether you would keep His commandments or not."

"Then we turned, and took our journey into the wilderness by the way of the Red Sea, as the LORD spoke unto me: and we compassed mount Seir many days. And the LORD spoke unto me, saying, Ye have compassed this mountain long enough: turn you northward. And command thou the people, saying, Ye are to pass through the coast of your brethren the children of Esau, which dwell in Seir; and they shall be afraid of you: take ye good heed unto yourselves therefore: Meddle not with them; for I will not give you of their land, no, not so much as a footprint; because I have given to the land to Esau as his possession." (Deut. 2:1-5)

Oftentimes, many people misinterpret when God seems to be moving in a new way. In the book of Acts, they thought the apostles were drunk on Pentecost. Hanna was accused of being drunk. David's motives were questioned when facing Goliath. God usually allows your loyalties to be challenged in light of His purposes. God's thoughts are not our thoughts neither His ways, our ways.

He alone, is God. We are not to worship any other person, place, or thing. Man looks on the outward appearance, but God looks at the heart. We need to get our hearts checked and perform an absolute heart search on our hearts to see if there is anything in us that needs to be removed. David said, "Search my heart, oh, God, and see if there be any wicked way in me."

Exodus 24 - Turn - וּפְנוּ (pə·nū) verb - Qal - Imperative - masculine plural

Strong's Hebrew 6437: 1) to turn 1a) (Qal) 1a1) to turn toward or from or away 1a2) to turn and do 1a3) to turn, decline (of day) 1a4) to turn toward, approach (of evening) 1a5) to turn and look, look, look back or at or after or for 1b) (Piel) to turn away, put out of the way, make clear, clear away 1c) (Hiphil) 1c1) to turn 1c2) to make a turn, show signs of turning, turn back 1d) (Hophal) to be turned back.

The North: Bible students have suggested that the north is a symbol of the permanent or the eternal, perhaps because the polar stars were permanently visible in the sky. It is the place of God's celestial dwelling (Isa. 14:13) and from which His glory descends (Job 37:22) with blessings or judgments (Eze. 1:4). He is the true King of the North. But the north—represented by the left hand—is also a symbol of disaster. The enemy of God's people came from the north (Jer. 1:14, 15; Eze. 38:6), bringing destruction. In a sense, the enemy was the false king of the north who tried to usurp God's role and is finally destroyed by the Lord (Zeph. 2:12; Dan. 11:21-45).

North: Tsafon, Smol. In the promise to Jacob, the north, tsafon, is the only direction whose name corresponds to the modern Hebrew word. Tsafon means "hidden" as it is the direction in which you will never see the sun. (The authors of the Bible were northern-hemisphere-centric.)The word tza•fon is more than just a mere direction. The root of this word is tza•fan, which means code, encode, cypher (or cipher).

Many came to believe that a power greater than ourselves could restore us to sanity.

Disillusionment, loss of faith, self-sufficiency, intellectualism, and defiance are all glaring character flaws of the addict.

Restore us to sanity - 1 Peter 5:10, "And the God of all grace, who called you to his eternal glory in Christ, after you have suffered a little while, will himself restore you and make you strong, firm and steadfast." (NIV)

Restore - return someone, or something, from a condition, place, or position; to repair or renovate to its original condition. You were originally created good, not corrupt. Jeremiah states, "For I know the plans that I have for you, plans that are good and not evil to give you a hope and a future."

Repair - to fix me and put right the damaged relationships, or unwelcome situations.

Renovation - the art of renewing; to restore to a form; a better state by cleansing, repairing, and rebuilding. The process of improving a broken, damaged, outdated structure and making it new or bringing it back to life.

Mark 5:15, "When they came to Jesus, they saw the man who had been possessed by the legion of demons sitting there, clothed and in his right mind; and they were afraid." (BSB)

Sanity means to have a sound mind, or judgment free from mental defects, mental disease mental damage, or mental distortion.

I once heard restoration explained as the 4 Rs: Replace, Renew, Revive, and Return.

Replace: God replaces our hearts of stone with hearts of flesh. —Ezekiel 36:26

Renew: By focusing on the Bible, our minds can be continually renewed. —Romans 12:2

Revive: Through the resurrection of Jesus, we are given new, everlasting life. —Romans 6:4

Return: Through the saving work of Jesus on the cross, we are reunited with God. —Romans 5:10, "For if, when we were enemies of God, we were reconciled to Him through the death of His Son, how much more, having been reconciled, shall we be saved through His life!" (BSB)

Mark 1:3, "The voice of the one crying in the wilderness, 'Prepare ye the way of the Lord, make his paths straight.'"

Voices are so important to humans. They are the medium through which we do a lot of communicating with the outside world: our ideas, of course, and also our emotions and our personality.

Here are five different types of communication:

- **Oral communication** means word of mouth which is verbal, using words. Verbal communication is the most common type of communication. Presentations, speeches, and dialogues are all examples of oral communication. Although words are used to communicate the message. For thousands of years, the Bible has been passed on as oral stories. The promises God gave to Abraham, Isaac, and Jacob were passed down by the Jewish people for generations before Genesis was ever written. The prophets God sent to Israel and Judah delivered oral messages to the people. Proverbs 15:1, "A soft answer turns away wrath, but a harsh word stirs up anger." Ephesians 4:29, "Let no corrupt communication proceed out of your mouth, but that which is good to the use of edifying, that it may minister grace unto the hearers."

- **Nonverbal communication** is the act of conveying information without the use of words. Nonverbal communication occurs through facial expressions, gestures, body language, tone of voice, and other physical indications of mood, attitude, approbation, and so forth, some of which may require knowledge of the culture or subculture to understand. God can impart into you more when you are quiet and listening. Faith comes by hearing and hearing by the word of God. We need grace to discern a matter. Proverbs 6:12-13, "A worthless person, a wicked man, goes about with crooked speech, winks with his eyes, signals with his feet, points with his finger." Genesis 3:8-9, "And they heard the voice of the Lord God walking in the garden in the cool of the day: and Adam and his wife hid themselves from the presence of the Lord God amongst the trees of the garden. And the Lord God called unto Adam, and said unto him, Where art thou?"

- **Contextual communication** is the context that results in a basic understanding of the situation in which the communication is taking place, and the factors that influence the communication also become quite important in this respect. As the term suggests, contextual communication is the transfer of information by deriving maximum information from the context, in this case, the customer. In the digital realm, this setting could be visual, physical, or analytical data. In the book of Genesis 39:23, God was with Joseph.

- **Active Listening** the practice of engaging closely with what a speaker is saying and indicating understanding, typically by asking relevant questions, using gestures, and summarizing; it is the practice of preparing to listen, observing what verbal and non-verbal messages are being sent, and then providing appropriate feedback for the sake of showing attentiveness to the message being presented.[1] This form of listening conveys a mutual understanding between speaker and listener. Speakers receive confirmation their point is coming across effectively, and listeners absorb more content and understanding by being engaged. Proverbs 18:13, "To answer before listening- that is folly and shame." 1 Samuel 3:10, "The LORD came and stood there, calling as at the other times, "Samuel! Samuel!" Then Samuel said, "Speak, for your servant is listening."

- **Visual communication**. Visual communication in the workplace or business is to share ideas and provide information for specific points that need to be emphasized for the success of the business or corporate setting for an advantage of their success. Joel 2:28, "And it shall come to pass afterward, that I will pour out my spirit upon all flesh; and your sons and your daughters shall prophesy, your old men shall dream dreams, your young men shall see visions." Habakkuk 2:2, "And the LORD answered me, and said, 'Write the vision, and make it plain upon tables, that he may run that reads it."

Write the vision here, in these remaining pages...make it plain...
make it clear...what is the vision, the plan, His purposes, that the
LORD has placed inside of you?

What has He whispered to you?

Write it out, make it plain, and be obedient to the LORD in His
Word, knowing that He loves you with an everlasting love...

Kevin B. Graham

God Whispers

www.ingramcontent.com/pod-product-compliance
Lightning Source LLC
Chambersburg PA
CBHW031236120626
46545CB00003B/1137